TEACHING PALLIATIVE CARE:

ISSUES AND IMPLICATIONS

Dr. Roderick D. MacLeod
Dr. Chris James
Editors

Kim Rogers
Editorial Assistant

Patten Press
Newmill, Penzance

First published in Great Britain by the Patten Press, The Old Post Office, Newmill, Penzance , Cornwall TR20 4XN for the Macmillan Education Centre of the Dorothy House Foundation, Bath.

ISBN 1 872229 30 1

Typeset at the Patten Press. Printed & bound at The Book Factory, London N7 7AH.

CONTENTS

FOREWORD

FOREWORD

This monograph outlines the thoughts and discussions heard during a seminar held in Bath on 19th July 1993 entitled 'Teaching Palliative Care : Issues and Implications'. The day was organised by Roderick MacLeod and Chris James with the support of the Macmillan Education Centre of the Dorothy House Foundation, Bath, and participants were invited from a background either in education or palliative care. The day provided an opportunity for those involved to explore some of the relevant issues in this field and to have an opportunity to discuss those issues with participants both from different disciplines and different countries. By providing a structure to the day we hoped to encourage people to think of ways forward in the different themes discussed.

The monograph provides an account of keynote addresses and discussions and summaries from the three interest groups who looked not only at what has happened in the past and is happening now, but also what might develop in the future. The final chapter 'Future Considerations' gave us an opportunity to highlight what we feel were significant areas for future consideration.

We would like to express our thanks to the following for their considerable support:

Bath Spa Hotel, Bath

Glaxo Oncology Group

Janssen Pharmaceutical Ltd

Dorothy N. Garrett, International Hospice Institute

Geraldine Goodacre, Macmillan Education Centre

Jill Griffiths, Macmillan Education Centre

RDM & CRJ

1.

THE CONTEXT OF EDUCATION IN PALLIATIVE CARE

Roderick MacLeod and Chris James

This 'Introduction' section has three purposes. The first is to outline the background to the seminar by briefly exploring some of the important issues in palliative care education which represent the context in which the seminar took place. The second purpose is to explain the structure of the day and our intentions for it and to provide some information about those who gave the keynote addresses and those who facilitated the discussion groups. The third purpose is to outline the structure of this monograph.

The context

The nature of palliative care

Over the last three decades palliative care has emerged as an identifiable specialty that embraces many disciplines in the field of health care provision. The World Health Organisation (WHO) defines palliative care as:

"the active total care of patients at a time when their disease is no longer responsive to curative measures and when control of pain and other symptoms and of psychological, social and spiritual problems is paramount. The goal of palliative care is the highest possible quality of life for the patient and family" (WHO, 1990).

Palliative care affirms life and regards dying as a normal process. It emphasises relief from pain and other distressing symptoms; integrates the physical, psychological and spiritual aspects of patient care; offers a support system to help the patient live as actively as possible until death and gives a support system to help the family during the patient's illness and in bereavement. Palliative care stresses advanced planning rather than crisis intervention.

1

The increasing need for palliative care

The vast majority of those receiving palliative care have cancer. The need for palliative care will increase in all countries over the coming years. National projections in the UK, for example, indicate that by the year 2000 the cumulative increase in the incidence of cancer could be between 13% and 20% (Stjernsward et al, 1992).

The development of palliative care as a specialty has seen the burgeoning of centres where palliative care is practised. For example, in the United Kingdom, by January 1993 there were 193 in-patient units, in addition to 216 hospitals with support teams or support nurses, and over 200 day care hospices for palliative care, either free-standing or attached to hospice in-patient units or teams (St. Christopher's Hospice Information Service, 1993).

As the need for palliative care increases so does the need for palliative care education. However, the nature of palliative care means that teaching and learning about it are complex and problematic (James and MacLeod, 1993).

Palliative care as an emerging specialty

The relatively short life so far of palliative care means that there is not a long history of academic exploration and scrutiny. The essence of hospice care is the provision of 'good quality' care addressing emotional, physical, social and spiritual needs of patients and carers but this type of care is often ill-defined and difficult to measure. There is a danger that because of the relative ease of measurement, physical elements may take priority over some other dimensions that make up the totality of care. Because of the difficulty in measuring those dimensions, there is, for some, a difficulty in conceptualisation. Academic medicine is so often assessed in quantitative terms and qualitative evaluation is difficult for some to identify with.

The palliative care educator is faced with the challenge of educating carers about a domain of practice the limits, objectives and nature of which are not clearly defined nor unequivocally agreed by the different practitioners involved. Because of this, programmes developed for teaching palliative care have been difficult to evaluate and published evidence is scarce.

2

The importance of symptom control

The development of expertise in the field of pain control has given a certain credibility to the discipline of palliative care despite the fact that pain control is still inadequately understood by many. Significant in-roads into this lack of understanding have been made by the WHO through their cancer pain relief programme (WHO, 1990).

Although pain control is important, it is worth noting that there are symptoms, as equally distressing as pain, for example breathlessness. These other symptoms may be just as common but have not attracted the same degree of interest or investigation. This may illustrate a further difficulty, that of contextualisation. These symptoms can appear in dimensions, in extent and in settings very different from a practitioner's previous experience. Severity, persistence and multiplicity are often the hallmarks of difficult symptoms at the end of life. If we return to the symptom of breathlessness, the previously validated scales for breathlessness all involve a certain degree of activity whereas breathlessness at the end of life can occur with speech or with minimal movement. The increased severity of these symptoms can cause considerable distress to the practitioner which in turn has the potential to distort the frame within which he or she makes judgements. For the palliative care educator there are many challenges here. Teaching must acknowledge the true complexity of symptom control of the terminally ill, recognise the importance of reflecting on and learning from experience, and allow opportunities for collaboration between practitioners.

Palliative care is not curative in the accepted sense

If the 'medical model' of illness is used to conceptualise palliative care it cannot be viewed as 'curative' in the accepted sense. Although it can be argued that all care is essentially 'palliative', in many medical interventions an outcome considered to be only palliative would be neither desirable nor satisfactory. 'To make well' in a conventionally accepted sense is likely to be an important motivation of those entering the medical and nursing professions; palliative care may not satisfy that motivation. This issue can present educators with complicated problems. For example, Feifer (1965) has suggested that medical students enter medicine precisely because of their desire to overcome a greater than average fear of death. Much has been written about the training of medical students and the 'certainty' which is engendered in that training (see for example Atkinson 1984; Fox 1957). On the wards and in much of their practice medical students encounter patients who have *'some well established, observable and relatively discreet pathology'* (Atkinson, 1984, p.951). In palliative medicine the pathology is undoubtedly present but so many other different facets appear or develop that uncertainty is enhanced. Current teaching in palliative medicine may well compound this problem by concentrating on the pathological aspects rather than on the individual as a whole.

Of course, the non-curative nature of palliative care may not be an issue for all of those involved, some of whom will have made a deliberate choice to care for terminally ill patients. However, it remains an important issue to be addressed in palliative care education together with other aspects such as the uncertainty of palliative care and the anxiety developed in the carer during her or his work.

Responding to individual needs

Responding to the particular needs of individual patients is fundamental to all medical care. However, the palliative care needs of the terminally ill patient are likely to be more wide-ranging than the needs of the non-terminally ill. In the process of palliative care, those needs will be responded to by individuals and by teams of different kinds. The range of individuals in those teams can oblige palliative care to be multidisciplinary and therefore multiprofessional in a way that other forms of medical care are not. The relatively restricted nature of many other forms of medical care, such as orthopedics, encourages a greater clarity of the role definition of the carers. Arguably, in these cases roles are more likely to match professional titles, and doctors and nurses in those situations are likely to be clearer about the boundaries of their professional roles. Within hospice care teams, occasional difficulties can arise in the grey area between medical and nursing functions as roles become blurred. The potential for role confusion or overlap is exacerbated in palliative care because the palliative care team may include a chaplain, social worker, physiotherapist, and occupational therapist in addition to conventionally defined doctors and nurses. The nature of palliative care and the variety of patient needs may challenge established hierarchies of status and the wide-ranging and varying needs of individuals mean that team roles will vary also.

Collaborative practice in palliative care

The practice of collaboration in teams has important implications for palliative care practice and education. Very importantly for the palliative care practitioners, there is the difficulty of sharing knowledge in the care setting. The complexity of the palliative care knowledge and its nature as a basis for action presents a particular challenge for those faced with the task of explaining aspects of palliation to others. This task may be yet more challenging because those 'others' in the team may not hold the 'framework for understanding' which is essential if that sharing of understanding is to take place. This may be because that framework is not yet developed, in the case of a student, or may be of a different kind as may be the case of the different members of a multiprofessional team. Meyer (1993) in a study of lay participation in care has outlined many of the problems relating to such participation and highlights the fact that, despite an apparently multidisciplinary team approach, various factors inhibit a collaborative approach to care. Most professional groups within such teams have been encouraged to identify and adopt a task-orientated or problem-solving approach to care whereas a more patient-centred approach (as espoused by most palliative care organisations) demands the development of more flexibility and supportive skills to foster individual patient care. In order that they are at their most effective and efficient this flexibility and skill should be developed in an interdisciplinary team.

The implications here for palliative care education are significant. The task is not one restricted solely to teaching palliative care but encompasses encouraging those involved: to understand fully their theories and bases for action; to be able to articulate those to others; and to develop in other carers frameworks for the understanding of practice. There is also the important task of developing collaborative practice so that carers are able to work effectively in teams and to understand the nature of their role within them. This issue is discussed further in the final part of the paper.

The emotional and psychological demands of palliative care

The emotional and psychological demands of palliative care are immense. The distance and detachment perhaps possible and even desirable in other forms of medicine are not so in palliative care. Indeed, there is a case for arguing the opposite, that is, in palliative care, engaging with the patient is a central and essential feature.

Hafferty (1991) has identified specific problems in medical training relating to 'feelings' inculcated during that training. He identified a variability with respect to 'affect' that can be traced to the tension between medicine's dominant values of detachment and distance and lay values of concern and affectivity. His study identified individuals who were wrestling with these concepts and who were unable to resolve the emotional difficulty of practising clinical medicine. In Hafferty's study, these individuals were unlikely to find any formal institutional support for their continued efforts to

5

maintain a sense of 'self' as a sensitive, caring and reflexive social being. Over time he suggested, it was easy to tire of the struggle. Of course, for all those committed to palliative care, to 'tire of the struggle' to be caring and sensitive as a consequence of the demands made would be a negation of the principles of practice of palliative care. It is however not adequate to leave it at that. This issue must feature in palliative care education so that practitioners can understand and cope with the often intense demands made on them.

The wide range of settings for palliative care

As palliative care emerges as an important field in medical care and as a conceptualisation of it emerges also, it is becoming increasingly apparent that palliative care takes place in a wide range of settings. These settings include, for example, hospitals, hospices, nursing homes and patients' homes. This has implications for the contextualisation of the professional knowledge held and used by palliative carers. These aspects of the context are not concerned solely with location (that is, place) but with its physical features, important but unwritten rules and routines, significant aspects of its culture and so on. Interacting with this are the contextual aspects of the patient's medical and care needs. These will include where the patient lives, the quality of support available to the patient in her/his home and a range of other factors. The knowledge on which judgements about the most appropriate location for palliative care is therefore an important element of palliative care knowledge and addressing this is an important aspect of palliative care education.

The antecedents of professional knowledge

As in other professional activities, such as teaching, (see, for example, Calderhead, 1988; Connelly and Clandinin, 1988) the palliative care practitioner's prior experience is likely to have a significant impact on individuals' practice and their professional development. Prior experience is likely to shape the way they learn, their learning needs, their perspective of palliative care, what they consider to be important priorities, how they relate to others involved in the care process, and their ability to articulate and explain the bases for their actions. Importantly, prior experience will also be a significant influence on their motivation to care for the terminally ill. Although this may be obvious it can be easily ignored in the educational process. Prior experience must represent an important starting point and should be continually re-visited as part of the professional development process.

6

In order to achieve a better understanding of palliative care one approach would be to respond directly to the challenges outlined in the previous sections. That is particular 'problems' in palliative care could be identified, separated out and analysed and then made the focus of educational activities. This vision of palliative care is not an appropriate one because it fails to do justice to its holistic character with its multiplicity of interrelated, interconnected and dynamic facets of a personal, technical, practical, moral, social, emotional and spiritual kind. Any denial of this vision has two drawbacks.

Firstly, it can lead to a technologising of palliative care education. This technical approach views palliative care education as a set of discreet instrumental responses to the different 'parts' of palliative care. This view has been a characteristic of some published curricula (see for example, Association for Palliative Medicine and the Royal College of General Practitioners, 1993).

The second drawback is that it can lead to a bureaucratic response to learning about palliative care. Within this bureaucratic response, teaching would be founded on a deficit model. It would be characterised, for example, by the reliance on didactic approaches which sought to transmit knowledge about palliative care to those 'who did not know' or by an over-emphasis on behavioural objectives for learning activities which promote a de-personalised and technical view of palliative care. It is not likely that such simplistic approaches will meet the needs of the palliative care learner. Despite this, MacLeod (1992), reported that didactic approaches dominate medical palliative care teaching practice in the UK with 66% of the most common topics being taught by means of lectures. This may in part be explained by the lack of training of medical palliative care teachers since MacLeod (1992) reported that only one sixth of the respondents in his survey had received any training in teaching methods and strategies. The criticism of lectures and didactic approaches in palliative care education is not saying that aspects of palliative care cannot be represented by factual knowledge. It is, however, asserting that palliative care is best characterised by forms of knowledge which are personal and shared, which communicate real meaning through interpretation, and which have moral and spiritual dimensions. Likewise the criticism of a behavioural objective approach to education in palliative care is not based on an assertion that educational activities should not have intentions or purposes. It is simply recognising that the complexity of many aspects of palliative care make it impossible to predict and specify the nature of the educational outcomes in any prescriptive way. Methods of education in palliative care education must match the true characterisation of palliative care knowledge and, possibly more importantly, must recognise and draw upon the ways in which practitioners have actually acquired their own expertise. An important implication arising from this is that more research is required into the processes of palliative care education; research which focuses on questions of the kind 'how do people learn palliative care and how can this learning be improved?'. It was to address questions of this kind that the seminar was held.

About the seminar

Purposes and intentions

The overall purpose of the seminar was to examine the issues surrounding the teaching of palliative care and to explore the implications of past experience for the future development of both teaching and learning.

From the outset, the intention was to draw to the seminar a wide range of practitioners not only from the UK but also from overseas. We were helped in this regard by the organisers of the Ninth Annual Symposium of the International Hospice Institute, which immediately preceded the seminar, who disseminated information about the seminar to the participants of the Symposium. We considered that encouraging a range of participants was in keeping with the nature of palliative care and would provide the broadest possible perspective on the issues. In the event this was achieved (see List of Contributors, page 54) and the seminar benefitted considerably as a result.

The rationale for the overall shape of the seminar was as follows. There would be 'keynote' inputs at the start by acknowledged experts in the field to provide an overview of palliative care education and to review the nature of professional knowledge and professional learning. These inputs would be followed by interest groups each of which would discuss one of these important themes:

--multiprofessional learning;

--teaching palliative care tutors to teach;

--problems in conceptualising palliative care.

The tasks of these groups would be to review the current state of play and to explore future considerations. The choice of themes followed wide consultation with professional colleagues. The themes were considered to be the most important, the most pressing and the most problematic.

8

Following a report from the interest groups, there would be an opportunity for all participants to contribute to a general discussion. The keynote speakers who had given the overviews at the start of the day would respond to the outcomes of the day.

The overview of teaching in palliative care was given by Neil MacDonald who is the Alberta Cancer Foundation Professor of Palliative Medicine in the Department of Medicine in Alberta, Canada. James Calderhead who gave an overview of professional knowledge and professional learning is Professor of Education at the University of Bath.

The seminar programme

The programme was as follows.

09.00 Arrivals

09.30 Opening remarks - Roderick MacLeod, Medical Director, Dorothy House Foundation, Bath, UK.

09.40 'Teaching Palliative Care: a Structural Overview' - Neil MacDonald, Professor of Palliative Medicine, University of Alberta, Canada.

10.10 'Professional Learning' - James Calderhead, Professor of Education, University of Bath, Bath, UK.

10.40 Coffee

11.00 Interest groups

--'Multiprofessional Learning' - facilitated by Mary Thomas, Lecturer in Medical Education, University of Dundee, UK.

--'Teaching Palliative Teachers to Teach' - facilitated by Colin Coles, Senior Lecturer in Medical Education, University of Southampton, UK.

--'Problems in Conceptualising Palliative Care' - facilitated by Suzanne Skevington, Senior Lecturer in Psychology, University of Bath, UK.

13.00 Lunch

14.00 Reports from the morning session led by Chris James, Lecturer in Education, University of Bath, UK.

14.30 Interest groups - 'Where are we going?'

15.45 Tea

16.00 Reports from the interest groups

16.30 General discussion

17.00 Response from the keynote speakers

About this monograph

What the reader of this monograph will find is a transcript of the two keynote addresses followed by short articles from each of the discussion group sessions which focussed on the three themes outlined above. The overview of the group work is presented by a reporter from each of the small groups with comment from the group facilitators. There is a summary of the outcomes of the discussions of the interest groups and then the observations of the keynote speakers, Neil MacDonald and James Calderhead are presented in summary form. The book ends with a final reflective observation from the organisers of the seminar where future considerations are discussed.

References

Association for Palliative Medicine and the Royal College of General Practitioners (1993) *Palliative Medicine Curriculum.* Southampton, Association for Palliative Medicine.

Atkinson, P (1984) Training for certainty. *Social Science and Medicine,* 19 (9), 949-956.

Calderhead, J (1988) *Teachers' Professional Learning.* London, Falmer.

Connelly, M F and Clandinin, D J (1988) *Teachers as Curriculum Planners: Narratives of Experience.* New York, Teachers' College Press.

Feifer, H (1965) Death and dying: attitudes of patient and doctor. *Group for the Advancement of Psychiatry,* 5 (2), 632-641.

Fox, R (1957) Training for uncertainty. In Merton, R K (Ed) *The Student Physician,* Cambridge, Harvard University Press.

Hafferty, F W (1991) *Into the Valley: Death and the Socialisation of Medical Students.* New Haven, Yale University Press.

James, C R and MacLeod, R D (1993) The problematic nature of education in palliative care. *Journal of Palliative Care,* 9 (4), 5-11.

MacLeod, R D (1992) *Teaching Postgraduate Palliative Medicine.* Master of Medical Education Thesis, Dundee, University of Dundee.

Meyer, J (1993) Lay participation in care: a challenge for multidisciplinary teamwork. *Journal of Interprofessional Care,* 7 (1), 57-66.

St Christopher's Hospice Information Service (1993) *Directory of Hospice Services.* Sydenham, St Christopher's Hospice Information Service.

Stjernsward, J, Koroltchouk, V, and Teoh, N (1992) National policies for cancer pain relief and palliative care. *Palliative Medicine,* 6, 273-276.

World Health Organisation (1990) *Cancer Pain Relief and Palliative Care.* Technical Report Series 804, Geneva, World Health Organisation.

References

Association for Palliative Medicine and the Royal College of
General Practitioners (1993) *Palliative Medicine Curriculum*.
Southampton: Association for Palliative Medicine.

Aranson, P. (1994) Transcripts workshop. *Some Stance and Sta-
diums*, 10(9), pp. 353–

Calderhead, J. (1989) *Teachers' Professional Learning*. London: Falmer.

Carroll, J. M. and Schneider, E. (2000) *Learning from Orientation
Patterns in Learning*. New York: Teachers College
p.

Dreyfus, H. (1979) Teaching and the acquisition of nature and action.
Computerised Education Review, 16(3), pp. 92–97.

Eraut, R. (1994) Teaching for nurse lecturers in Nursing Research (ed.) *Nurse
Studies*. Basingstoke: Harcourt Brace University Press.

Faulkner, W. (ed.) (1994) ... ... *A Course on ... and Documentation*
Medical Students. Winchester: John University Press.

Jones, A. P. and Anderson, F. C. (1993) The implementation group of
undergraduate palliative care curriculum for learning. *Nurse Education*, ? pp. 3–

MacCalmont, C. (1997) ... ... *Nurse ... ... care Palliative Education*.
Master of Medical Education thesis, Dundee: University of Dundee.

Moyer, A. (1994) Nurse participation in a ... a ... nurse for palliative
... support a network. *Journal of ... Integrative Nursing Care*, 2(?) pp. ?–

St Christopher's Disease Education Research (2000) *Directory of
Hospice Services: Systematic Classification and ... 2000*. London:
Service.

Sepulveda, F., Karbashvili, V. and Teoh, N. (1992) National
policies for cancer health in relief and palliative ... . *Palliative Medicine*, 6, 227–236.

World Health Organisation (1990) *Cancer Pain Relief and Palliative
Care. Technical Report Series 804*. Geneva: World Health Organisation.

2.

TEACHING PALLIATIVE CARE:
A STRUCTURAL OVERVIEW

Neil MacDonald

Introduction

I am an oncologist by background. I became involved in palliative care through the influence of a colleague, Balfour Mount, with whom I trained at McGill at Montreal. I directed a cancer centre in the 1970s and early 1980s and I recognised that we oncologists were not able, despite our best efforts, to offer sufficient assistance to our cancer patients who went on to die of their disease. I went to work with Balfour Mount for a period and then returned to the University of Alberta with the goal of integrating principles of palliative care into our system of cancer care. That is the pulpit I preach from, and my homily expresses the need for integration of palliative medicine into the main-stream of oncology and medical practice.

I am going to start with a quote from Dr Jan Stjernsward, Chief of the World Health Organisation Cancer and Palliative Care Unit. Dr Stjernsward states:

"nothing would have more immediate effect on quality of life and relief of suffering, not only for cancer patients but also for their families, than implementing the knowledge that's accumulated in the field of palliative care".

We have available an excellent integrated interdisciplinary approach to the care of patients with advanced disease and we have developed a wealth of educational material and strategies to convey that approach but our task remains to move out from the cocoon in which I think palliative care still exists and to use the expertise that we have to influence the broader community of health professionals. I will use illustrations from oncology to demonstrate that our work is only partly done. Examples include:

1. A report from the Sloan-Kettering Cancer Institute indicating that lung and colon cancer patients in mid-trajectory of illness have an appreciable incidence of pain interfering with work, sleep and

enjoyment of life in a substantial percentage of cases. Nevertheless, in many cases the suffering is not recognised and appropriate analgesic therapy is not offered (Portenoy, 1992).

2. Using an example from the European literature, Dr Fossa recently provided data on the problems encountered by oncologists in determining the true functional ability of their patients. In this study, approximately one third of patients who were either confined to bed or only able to get out of bed for a limited period of time were assigned functional status ratings by physicians suggesting that they were fully ambulant or able to move around with only minor degrees of impairment (Fossa et al, 1990).

3. In Australia, there is evidence that medical students do not feel that they are adequately prepared in palliative care at the time of their graduation from medical school (Smith et al, 1991) while in Canada we have data suggesting that, despite all our educational efforts, many physicians continue to use inappropriate analgesics (Flynne, 1993).

These few examples are drawn from medical practice in developed countries where the principles of pain management have been well established and, we may have thought, well taught for many years.

Why, then, have not the principles of pain management and palliative medicine more clearly informed medical practice?

Part of the reason for this gap in what is taught and what is practised relates to the continued isolation of many palliative care programs from the mainstream of medical care. I have used cancer as an example, but I believe that similar examples may be found which apply to other chronic disorders.

We have many first rate palliative care programs but most of them are still concerned with a select group of patients, generally with cancer, toward the end of their life. While these focal points of excellence are providing a superb warm envelope of interdisciplinary care for a measured number of people they are not yet sufficiently influencing the care received by the broader community of cancer patients, AIDS patients, and other patients with chronic diseases which will ultimately take their life.

I believe, strongly, that palliative care should be more closely integrated into overall disease control programs. Using cancer as an example we may look upon cancer control as having four phases.

1. Prevention of occurrence (example - anti-smoking programs).

2. Prevention of invasive cancer (example - pap tests).

13

3. Prevention of death or severe morbidity (surgery, radiotherapy, chemotherapy).

4. Prevention of suffering (MacDonald, 1991).

Palliative care is concerned with the fourth phase, the prevention of suffering. Even where palliative care is well integrated into cancer control programs, the vast majority of palliative care activities are concerned with dying cancer patients and their families. However, the concerns of palliative care should extend beyond the final days of life and should more clearly inform the third phase of cancer control, during which time patients with life threatening cancers will be receiving aggressive anti-cancer care. In this phase, the patterns of pain, psychological distress and other symptoms which may cause a crescendo of suffering at the end of life will often become established. It is not simply rhetoric to say that principles of palliative care should be applied as early in its trajectory of illness as possible. My nursing colleagues suggest that psycho-social problems of cancer patients often have their genesis early in the course of disease and that problems at the end of life will be accentuated if these psycho-social problems were ignored at an earlier time.

With respect to pain, there is good research data showing that uncontrolled pain results in alterations in the patterns of neuro-transmission in the central nervous system, with activation of previously silent pathways transmitting the pain message. These changes can lead to a situation whereby chronic pain becomes increasingly difficult to manage. For these reasons it is not sensible to suddenly address pain or psycho-social distress towards the end of life and to regard these issues as lying in separate compartments from other aspects of cancer care. The integration of palliative care programs directly into cancer services, one hopes, can lead to a situation wherein pain and other distressful symptoms are managed in an impeccable fashion at whatever time during the course of illness they may occur.

I believe that we need to do more than preach to the converted at palliative care conferences and to simply develop more print and audio-visual educational material on palliative care. These initiatives are important but must be combined with structural changes in our educational approaches which will result in not only diffusion of palliative care principles widely through medical communities but also lead to actual changes in practice patterns.

The conference organisers had asked me to talk about a 'structured approach to education'. I interpret a 'structured approach' as a framework in which strategies for the diffusion of palliative care education can successfully develop. I will provide a few illustrations

14

of what I believe to be essential components of the framework which we wish to see come into place. These include the following.

1. Recognition that education is primarily a university responsibility and that, as a corollary, palliative care must be established as a university discipline.

In a few universities in the English speaking world, palliative care has achieved academic recognition either through the introduction of Chairs in palliative medicine or the formation of divisions or departments of palliative medicine. Both of these approaches can provide an administrative structure within which palliative medicine can flourish. The case for palliative care education can be argued at the dean's and department director's tables while opportunities for liaison with other academic disciplines is enhanced.

2. The specific goals and objectives of palliative care education should be clearly stated in educational terms.

The publication of *The Canadian Palliative Care Curriculum* represents an example of an initiative in this sphere (MacDonald et al, 1993). This Curriculum addresses the specific attitudes, skills and knowledge which undergraduate medical students should possess at the time of graduation relevant to 22 problem areas including major symptoms, psycho-social distress, collaborative work with other health professionals, and home care planning. Two examples of this approach are contained in Appendix I and II.

3. Specific palliative care education programs should be introduced into the formal residency training programs for oncologists and family physicians.

Recent initiatives of the American Society of Clinical Oncology (ASCO) represent examples of work in this sphere. ASCO has formally stated that cancer pain education and research should receive a higher priority in oncology training. Tangible projects stemming from this philosophy include the recent publication of the *Cancer Pain Curriculum* (ASCO, 1992) and the organisation of a course manual and slides which complement the Curriculum. In the fall of 1993 the directors of 103 oncology training programs in the United States were invited to attend a symposium where the course syllabus on cancer pain was discussed and distributed. As a result of this initiative, ASCO hopes to 'teach the teachers' who, in turn, will then be able to return to their resident training programs with excellent teaching material readily enabling them to introduce teaching on cancer pain into their programs. An example of how we can use educational hierarchies to list resident responsibilities in one area, the use of anti-cancer therapy for symptom control, is outlined in Appendix III.

4. Physicians will be moved to learn about palliative care if patient assessment techniques in use pinpoint the degree of suffering which is experienced by their patients.

I earlier gave an example of first rate physicians who, perhaps because they were concentrating more on biologic issues related to cancer, failed to appreciate the functional limitations of their patients. If we can train our physicians to use simple objective assessment tools in their clinics, they will be more likely to recognise and address various elements of patient suffering which may not otherwise come to their attention. An example of a system which can be used in a clinic to further this goal is the *Edmonton Symptom Assessment Scheme* (Bruera, 1991). This Scheme uses a series of visual analogue scales and questions to provide measurable evidence of symptom distress. This information is particularly valuable as it is provided by patients following instruction in use of the form by nursing colleagues. If the patient provides the physician with a scale indicating that pain is at a level of eight or nine out of 10 or that anxiety is at similar levels, the physician must respond.

5. We must recognise that residents and physicians in practice are influenced to change practice patterns when they are able to observe examples of new approaches which have positively changed the course of their patients.

The organisation of formal palliative care consult teams within teaching institutions provides an admirable structure for demonstrating the principles of palliative care. In the course of doing a consultation and following up patients who, one hopes, will demonstrate the successful application of your consultation advice, an excellent educational experience is shared. The use of consults as impromptu and informal ward seminars may be enhanced through providing for colleagues, wherever possible, specific articles relevant to the points covered in the consult.

6. We should further encourage the integration of palliative care education for various professional groups with patient and family education.

Many palliative care units have developed first rate teaching material for families. As a result, educated families will now be able to interact in a more knowledgeable way with the attending health care professionals. This process, in turn, will require health professionals to be more clearly informed and aware of palliative care advances. Informed and concerned family groups can certainly stimulate initiatives and help to set the priorities for education.

The World Health Organisation is very conscious of the primacy of patient-family education in developing countries. Recently they have structured a small committee to develop the *Family Manual* for use in these countries. Ms Jo Hockley, a nurse clinician in palliative care in Britain, has been commissioned to write the first draft of the *Family Manual*.

7. Regulatory bodies should take steps to use their authority to improve the palliative care education of health professionals.

Students know our priorities for education as they are clearly outlined in the examinations which they must pass to further advance their medical careers. A higher priority for palliative care education should be reflected in an increased number of examination questions on our qualifying examinations.

The information obtained by regulatory agencies in the course of their activity should be used to provide a positive educational experience. For example, in North America, many states or provinces have triplicate prescription programs which are used to monitor physician prescribing patterns of opioids and other potential drugs of abuse. In Alberta, this program is operated by our College of Physicians and Surgeons. Every opioid prescription is ultimately entered into a College computer which can provide detailed information on the use of various opioids on a regional basis. We are planning to feed this information back to physicians and hospitals in the form of an educational letter which, we hope, will stimulate a review of opioid practice in certain areas. This project represents an example of a proactive initiative by a regulatory body, adding an educational component to its usual policing role.

Audit techniques for palliative care have been well established in Britain through the work of Higginson and McCarthy (1989) and others. Data gathered in the course of auditing palliative care programs can provide an excellent tool for influencing practice patterns.

Conclusion

In this talk I have reviewed components of an educational framework which can result in the assignment of a higher priority to palliative care education in our professional training programs. Will a higher profile translate into improved practice? While we cherish the belief that this process is axiomatic, increased use of medical audit techniques will enable us to more clearly relate outcome to process.

References

1. Portenoy, R. (1992) Pain in ambulatory patients with lung and colon cancer. *Cancer,* 70 (6), 1616-1624.

2. Fossa, S D, Aaronson, N K, Newling D, van Cangh, P J, Denis, L, Kurth, K-H, dePauw, M, and the members of the EORTC Genito-Urinary Group. (1990) Quality of life and treatment of hormone resistant metastic prostatic cancer. *European Journal of Cancer,* 26, 1133-1136.

3. Smith, W T, Tattersall, M H N, Irwig, L M and Langlands, A O (1991) Undergraduate education about cancer. *European Journal of Medicine,* 27 (11), 1448-1453.

4. Flynne, P (1993) College of Physicians and Surgeons of Alberta (personal communication).

5. MacDonald, N (1991) Palliative care - The fourth phase of cancer prevention. *Cancer Detection and Prevention,* (15) 3, 253-255.

6. MacDonald, N, Mount, B, Scott, J and Boston, W (1993) The Canadian Palliative Care Curriculum. *Journal of Cancer Education,* 8 (3), 197-201.

7. Ad Hoc Committee on Cancer Pain of the American Society of Clinical Oncology (1992) Cancer pain assessment and treatment curriculum guidelines. *Journal of Clinical Oncology,* 10 (12), 1976-1982.

8. Bruera, E, Kuehn, N, Miller, M J, Selmser, P and Macmillan, K (1991) The Edmonton Symptom Assessment System (ESAS): A simple method for the assessment of palliative care patients. *Journal of Palliative Care,* 7(2), 6-9.

9. Higginson, I and McCarthy, M. (1989) Measuring symptoms in terminal cancer: Are pain and dypsnoea controlled? *Journal of the Royal Society of Medicine,* 82, 264.

APPENDIX I

6.CONSTIPATION

ATTITUDE

To enable each student:

6.1 to recognise that 'the hand that writes the narcotic order should, unless there is a contraindication, write a laxative order';

6.2 to adopt the habit of regularly checking the rectum in patients who are badly constipated.

SKILL

To enable each student:

6.3 to classify commonly used laxatives and apply a protocol for the use of these agents in patients receiving narcotic analgesics or otherwise constipated;

6.4 to name and describe the types of enemas that may be employed and master a protocol for using enemas under appropriate circumstances.

KNOWLEDGE

To enable each student:

6.5 to describe the pathophysiology of altered bowel motility with emphasis on the effect of drugs on the bowel and the presence of an altered state of motility in patients with advanced cancer and other terminal illnesses;

6.6 to describe the signs and symptoms of severe constipation and faecal impaction.

APPENDIX II

HOME CARE OF DYING PATIENTS

ATTITUDE

To enable each student:

2.1 to recognise the special needs of patients and their families when they are being cared for at home: the emotional stress and physical exhaustion often suffered by family members; their need for support in their role as caregivers; their need for information; their need to know that the physician is accessible in times of crises;

2.2 to explain the importance of keeping in close touch with the Home Care nurse and responding promptly to her/his calls for assistance;

2.3 to explain the importance of making regular home visits in the terminal stage of the illness rather than waiting to be called;

2.4 to explain the importance of being available outside normal office hours for crises and at the time of the death. If not personally available, the importance of having a deputy who knows about the patient and is prepared to visit the home if needed.

SKILL

To enable each student:

2.5 to do a functional assessment of a patient at home;

2.6 to check all medications being taken by patient;

2.7 to assess stress level of family caregivers and invite questions and expressions of feeling;

2.8 to assess family function if opportunity arises.

KNOWLEDGE

To enable each student:

2.9 to describe the resources available for Home Care in the area of her/his practice;

2.10 to describe the responsibilities of physicians when death occurs in home.

APPENDIX III:

TRAINING GOALS

A. AWARENESS

1. Trainees will be aware of the possibilities for alleviating pain and other aspects of suffering through the use of anti-cancer therapies.

B.. ATTITUDE

1. Trainees will regard the assessment of pain and suffering as an essential, integral part of the evaluation process for deciding on the use of chemotherapy and measuring the outcomes achieved through the use of chemotherapy.

C. KNOWLEDGE

1. Trainees will be aware of the demonstrated and hypothetical mechanisms through which chemotherapy may influence cancer pain.

2. Trainees will also be familiar with patient-centred assessment techniques.

D. SKILLS

1. Trainees will develop the skill to include pain and supplementary quality of life evaluation into both their practice and their clinical trials design format.

2. Trainees will be skilled in using the guidelines for the use of chemotherapy to relieve pain and suffering and factor these guidelines into their overall judgement process with respect to recommendations on the use of anti-cancer therapies.

E. ART

1. Trainees will acquire the art of communication and use it to ensure that the goals of therapy are clearly understood by the patient, family members and the treating team.

F. QUEST

1. Trainees will appreciate the lack of knowledge on the effects of chemotherapy on many facets of cancer pain and symptom management.

2. Some will be stimulated to design research studies addressing changes in tumour biology induced by chemotherapy which account for the actions of chemotherapy in relieving pain and other symptoms.

3.

PROFESSIONAL LEARNING

James Calderhead

My own research interest lies in how student teachers learn to teach and how teachers' professional development might be better structured and supported to improve the quality of teaching and learning in schools. Whilst there are inevitably many differences between the work of teachers and those involved in palliative care, I suspect that there may well also be some similarities in the ways in which they learn their practice that are worthy of note. That of course is not a new idea. Donald Schon (1983) in his book *The Reflective Practitioner* makes the argument that there are several distinguishing features of all professionals' work. Whether they be lawyers, doctors, social workers, counsellors or teachers, there are some aspects of their work that are shared - - the fact, for instance, that they are faced with complex, 'messy' problems for which there are no straight-forward answers, and to which the practitioner must bring a wealth of particular knowledge and past experience to identify and test out possible solutions. A point that Donald Schon particularly emphasises is the way that professional practice has often been misconstrued in the past as a form of applied science. Frequently, professional training has presumed that there is a body of scientific or academic knowledge that the practitioner needs to master and that practice is largely a matter of putting this knowledge into action. Such a view greatly underestimates and undervalues the expertise of the practitioner and the craft knowledge that they have developed and which regularly informs their action.

What I would like to do in this paper is to outline some of the complexity of the knowledge and skills that are involved in professional practice and then go on to discuss some other dimensions of learning within professions, particularly those often referred to as the 'caring professions', and to generate some issues and questions about the nature and content of professional education. Most of my examples come from a teaching context, but I shall try to make links with more specific medical or palliative care contexts when I can.

Unfortunately, professional education has in the past often been construed in terms of training, in which professional development is seen as the acquisition of certain pre-defined knowledge and skills, and even this knowledge and skill has sometimes been conceptualised in extremely narrow terms. In the 1960s and early 70s, for instance, there was considerable interest in skill development involving such procedures as microteaching and microcounselling, and similar techniques were also employed in training for general practice and in psychiatry. In the case of microteaching, particular teaching skills were identified, such as starting a lesson, asking higher order questions, dealing with transitions from one activity to another. The teaching behaviours associated with these would be described in detail, and teachers would have the opportunity to practice them with small groups of students. Video feedback would enable them to evaluate and then refine their skills. The assumption was that the skills of effective teaching would be identified through classroom research linking teaching skills to children's achievement, student teachers could practice and develop these skills in 'safe' microteaching contexts and then go out into classrooms and be effective teachers. Indeed, this all seemed to work apart from the latter part! Bruce Joyce (1980), one of the early advocates of microteaching, discovered that teachers who had been trained in microteaching could, even 20 years later, return to college to demonstrate their learned skills in the microteaching laboratory, but displayed few signs of actually implementing these skills in the intervening 20 year period! Critics pointed towards the fact that what determines effectiveness in the classroom is probably not so much being able to ask higher order questions, for example, but knowing when to ask the right question of the right child at the right time. In other words, learning to teach is not just a behavioural activity, it involves substantial cognitive changes as well - teachers need to be able to interpret and evaluate what is going on and know when particular interventions may be appropriate.

That may seem an obvious statement to make but it is surprisingly often overlooked. Student teachers themselves often think of learning to teach in terms of simply picking up a few behavioural strategies. Willy Russell, the playwright of *Educating Rita* and *Shirley Valentine*, spoke recently in a radio interview about his own experiences as a student teacher and claims that he found most of his inspiration about teaching from reading books - in particular, he was greatly influenced by A.S. Neill's *Summerhill*, in which Neill describes how he translated many principles of psychotherapy into an educational context. Several of the particular school incidents that Neill recounts seemed highly appealing to Russell at the time. In one instance, for example, Neill describes an occasion when he is walking through the school grounds when he catches sight of a boy throwing a stone through a school window. Neill's initial reaction is to run over to the boy and give him a thorough telling off, but

24

on his way towards the boy he remembers that this is a child with serious social adjustment difficulties. He comes from a disturbed home background and he does not respond well to authority figures. Thinking quickly on his feet, Neill therefore walks up to the boy, picks up a stone and throws it through another window. Neill immediately commands the boy's respect, and uses his new status as a fellow deviant to further his relationship with the boy and eventually to discuss with him why people engage in destructive acts. This was a particularly memorable incident for Russell, because as a student teacher on his first playground duty, in an urban comprehensive in Liverpool, what should he encounter but a boy who threw a stone through a window. But he knew what to do. He'd read the book. He walked up to the boy, picked up another stone and threw it through the next window. What he hadn't bargained for, however, was that all the other kids in the playground seeing the teacher throw a stone through a window, decided it must be all right to join in!

Though the incident may be quite extreme, that kind of orientation towards learning to teach is not uncommon. Many student teachers think of learning to teach in terms of acquiring a number of rules or recipes, and believe that the function of teacher education is to equip them with a repertoire of these. In some research I carried out a few years ago, I tried to examine the kinds of recipes that experienced teachers might use and how these compared with those adopted by novice teachers. First of all, a list of common classroom critical incidents was developed with the assistance of some experienced teachers. Some of these concerned everyday managerial incidents, others were instructionally related, some simply concerned the normal social processes of relating to young children. Each incident was then presented to a sample of experienced teachers and to a group of student teachers half way through their initial teacher education course. After each incident, they were asked what more they needed to know about the situation in order to decide how to deal with it and what they would do.

In the case of experienced teachers, they would generally recall a series of typical incidents rather like the one presented to them and possibly suggest a few strategies that might be appropriate. Student teachers, on the other hand, usually gave much simpler responses.

For example, one of the incidents was 'The class is working quietly when a group of children start talking amongst themselves'. Experienced teachers frequently recounted six or more typical incidents of this kind - the class clown playing up, a child having a difficulty and asking around for help rather than approaching the teacher, a child not having listened to instructions and having to ask others what to do, a distraction like a wasp flying in through the window, or another teacher coming into the room, and so on.

In contrast, one student teacher responded to the same situation, saying: 'I'd wait until the noise reached an intolerable level than I'd tell them to shut up!' Interestingly, no amount of encouragement to expand on that answer could elicit any further elaboration.

The experienced teachers had more sophisticated perceptions of the critical incidents, and perceived the incidents in terms of an example of a possible range of typical incidents, and this range could be very readily brought to mind.

Interestingly, the experienced teachers did not provide anything like the same number of action solutions as they did variants of the problem. Indeed with some experienced teachers it was extremely difficult to get them to commit themselves to any particular response. One interpretation of this is that teachers' knowledge is not held in the form of action recipes for typical situations - 'this is what you do in x type situation'. Teachers use their memory of classroom incidents as a way of thinking about the particular problems they encounter. Their response to any particular situation may depend as much on their assessment of the children and context involved as the typifications they call to mind. When a group of children start making a lot of noise, for example, how the teacher responds may depend as much on what has happened immediately before, the type of lesson it is, the children involved, whether the children are working individually or in groups, and what has about to happen next, or how close it is to the end of the school day, and so on.

David Berliner (1988), looking at educators of different kinds, proposes a stage model in the development of teaching expertise, derived from Dreyfus and Dreyfus (1986) model of human expertise. This depicts five stages in the acquisition of expertise, beginning with the *novice stage* in which students seek rules and recipes to guide their actions. This is followed by the *advanced beginner stage* in which the teacher seeks contextual and strategic knowledge and begins to understand when rules are appropriate and when they might be broken. The third stage is that of *competence* in which the teacher is able to make conscious choices about what they are going to do and is able to monitor their own actions in the classrooms and adapt them to suit their chosen goals. The following stage is that of *proficiency*, marked by the use of intuition and know how. The teacher has come to perceive the classroom and their own actions in more holistic, inter-connected terms. They can automatically link their past experiences to present circumstances and develop an intuitive 'feel' for how things are going and what needs to be done next. Finally, there is the stage of *expert*, where the teacher and the task have become inseparable, the teacher's practice is characterised by a fluency and automaticity in which the teacher is rarely surprised and where the teacher is fully adapted to and in control of the situation. Whilst Berliner speculates that the novice stage might last for the first year of teaching, and that most teachers would reach a competent stage after three or four years, only a modest proportion of teachers, he suggests, move to the proficient stage and even fewer reach the expert stage.

You will be able to imagine more readily than I what those stages might correspond to in the case of palliative care.

Clearly, knowledge and practical skills are an important part of any professional development, and one of the contributions of research on professional practice has been to demonstrate that these can be much more complex and sophisticated than commonly believed. But there are also other aspects to professional learning that have recently been highlighted. These have also been demonstrated to be influential in shaping professional practice, and may well be of particular importance in palliative care.

Personal

As well as possessing important knowledge that influences their practice, practitioners may also hold attitudes, beliefs, and taken-for-granted ideas. They may have particular images in mind of good practice, various values and beliefs that shape how they think about their work, and various knowledge acquired from past life experiences that influences how they come to view themselves and what it is that they have to learn. In palliative care one might expect past medical experience to provide models for working with patients or certain ways of looking at the roles of medical practitioner, or certain ideas about patients and their lives. Such ideas can channel how the professional views their work, and these ideas, whether appropriate or not, may be fairly resistant to change. In addition, where the work involves establishing relationships with other people, the practitioner's personality is also intrinsically involved. How other people react to you as a person and one's own awareness of this become important areas for learning. Knowing oneself and understanding others and being able to establish appropriate relationships become significant areas to explore and develop awareness.

Socialisation

Care professionals frequently work within institutions which themselves exercise powerful ideological and physical constraints upon the way people work. In particular, the taken-for-granted beliefs and practices that dominate within an institution can strongly

27

influence how people think about their own particular practice, and good practice in general. Hospitals and medical schools have been well researched in this respect, in that there are strong socialising influences on the new young professional who becomes initiated into the medical culture (for example, Becker et al, 1961). Researchers have frequently identified the 'wash-out effect', whereby the norms of the institution strongly influence, or 'wash out' the practices and beliefs of the new recruit. There are political skills required here that frequently are not addressed in professional development - how does the relatively powerless novice negotiate within the institution to defend what they believe to be good practice or even to influence how the institution begins to construe good practice. There is an important issue of what might be done in professional training to equip trainees to cope with such pressures.

The moral dimension

In almost any professional activity that involves working with people, moral issues abound. I would think that in the area of palliative care, the moral dimension of the work is particularly significant. Issues about respecting patient's wishes, recognition of human dignity, religious issues and medical ethics may frequently create moral conflicts for the practitioner, which could potentially be quite anxiety provoking. Moral conflict can be particularly distressing for the novice since it is frequently implicit, and when it is unshared with others, the novice is left alone to agonise over the ambiguity and uncertainty that such dilemmas generally bring.

The reflective dimension

Part of becoming an effective professional in any field is being able to analyse and evaluate one's own experience and develop one's practice as a result. Donald Schon suggests that some of this reflection occurs in action as professionals use their knowledge to decide upon particular strategies, evaluating the effects of these strategies within their interactions with a client. Other aspects of reflection occur after the event as the practitioner reflects back on particular events and how they have been handled. Researchers on reflective practice have suggested that there are three different levels of reflection. A *technical level* focuses on whether actions meet pre-specified criteria, for example, has the patient been helped to achieve a particular target? Reflection at a *practical level,* on the other hand, is also concerned with whether the criteria are appropriate ones (for example, was helping the patient to achieve that target an appropriate strategy to adopt?). Whereas reflection at a *critical level* is more philosophical and is focused on what palliative care itself is about, and how this relates to actual care strategies.

Unfortunately, there is no one comprehensive, coherent theory of professional development that can help us understand how best to facilitate professional growth. Research on practitioners' knowledge and skill demonstrates how complex, sophisticated and context specific these are. Research on the development of professionals in various fields, however, also emphasises the influence of institutional cultures, past experiences, the implication of values and moral principles, and the metacognitive processes involved in reflection and learning in and from practice. Three clear implications can, however, be drawn from this work.

1. Professional practice is complex and multi-dimensional. It has cognitive, affective and behavioural components, although there is also a holistic quality about professional practice. We can try to describe it in terms of personal attributes, counselling skills, the handling of role conflicts, the reappraisal and influencing of medical culture - such an analysis highlights the complexity but also misses something of the way in which everything seems to hold together.

2. Learning in professional practice is different from the learning that typically occurs in higher education. Learning palliative care is different from learning physiology or pharmacology.

3. Learning in professional practice involves multiple forms of learning - learning to come to terms with one's own anxieties, fears and emotions is quite different from learning about counselling or analysing and evaluating one's own practice or identifying one's own preconceptions and beliefs. Learning in professional practice involves different types of learning - and these need further elaboration in order for us to develop a much fuller understanding of the processes of professional development and to know the kinds of experiences and support that might work to improve practice.

References

Becker, H S, Geer, B, Hughes, E, and Strauss, A (1961) *Boys in White*. Chicago, IL, University of Chicago Press.

Berliner, D (1988) The development of expertise in pedagogy. Paper presented at the annual meeting of the American Association of Colleges of Teacher Education, New Orleans, February, 1988.

Dreyfus, H L and Dreyfus, S E (1986) *Mind over Machine: The Power of Human Intuition and Expertise in the Era of the Computer*. New York: The Free Press.

Joyce, B (1980) *Flexibility in Teaching*. New York, Wiley.

Schon, D (1983) *The Reflective Practitioner*. San Francisco, Jossey Bass.

4.

TEACHING PALLIATIVE CARE TUTORS TO TEACH

Kim Rogers and Colin Coles

Introduction

This chapter discusses where we are now with respect to how we learn to teach and moves on to discuss ways forward to teaching palliative care tutors to teach. In outlining strategies and principles of palliative care teaching, it attempts to answer two central questions: how can we educate health professionals in palliative care to see their professional work in a different way and how do we teach the palliative care tutor to be an appropriate teacher, to educate the educators?

Where are we now?

In order to develop strategies and principles for teaching palliative care an examination of where and how the palliative care tutor has learned to teach needs first to be considered.

What is clear in this section, both here and in the research, is that the majority of those who are teaching palliative care have never had any formal teacher training themselves. How and where did they learn to teach?

Role models, both good and bad, were identified as a way of learning to teach. By watching others teach, one can identify how one wants and does not want to teach. Good and bad role models are useful then, in helping palliative care tutors to teach. Are role models a good way to learn to teach? Perhaps yes but learning from role models alone has its limitations which will be discussed later.

Some palliative care teachers have learned to teach from their students. In dealing with students' questions and difficulties, the teacher gains a deeper understanding of what he or she is trying to teach. Something which may seem obvious to the teacher may, in fact, be more complicated and multi-faceted. Hence questions from students allow teachers to develop their own understanding and knowledge of palliative care, which in turn, makes their own teaching more appropriate.

Some palliative care teachers have learned to teach from understanding theory. Theory is only part of what is needed to inspire and empower others to teach. Theory must be married with practice if it is to enable others to learn in appropriate ways.

Others have learned to teach by receiving formal feedback. Neil MacDonald outlines the teacher appraisal system at the School of Medicine, University of Alberta, Canada, where teachers are graded on a five point scale on the efficacy of their teaching. Evaluation or formal feedback, then, can give an indication of how to teach more appropriately. Teacher appraisal can also be informal, where colleagues and students give verbal feedback to the teacher.

Some have learned to teach by enrolling in short courses and workshops from City and Guilds or University update courses. Interestingly, many identified sharing journal articles and books with colleagues as a way of learning to teach.

What has been described up to this point, is informal learning and teaching. Indeed, when the question was put to this group of palliative care teachers, 'how many have received formal training in teaching'?, the answer, not surprisingly, was none. The difficulty then, is how to marry the informal learning and teaching with more formal training. One is not exclusive of the other. Both informal and formal processes are necessary in teaching palliative care tutors to teach. We might ask the question, how do we intervene in the formal teaching of tutors in an informal way?

Before looking at ways forward, there are a number of barriers which need to be overcome with respect to the combination of teacher and learner. Salient questions which need examination, are 'why do people resist learning' and 'why do people resist teaching'?

Barriers

There are many reasons why we resist learning and teaching. In order to teach others to become tutors, the right climate needs to be created first. A climate in which the fear of criticism and performance anxiety does not exist. Teaching is not normally considered a public activity. This is not its normally accepted culture. We need to hold the belief that we are able to do something positive in our medical care rather than admit we can do nothing. In short, fear and anxiety are barriers to learning and teaching. They can be overcome by demonstrating how successful one can be by not knowing something while at the same time staying in control.

Apart from creating the right climate for teaching and learning, the very models of what we teach need close examination. For example, teaching doctors to stand by a patient's bedside is wholly inappropriate in palliative care, as is teaching clinical nurse specialists to look after a dying patient's physical needs first and foremost. The models, or the ways in which doctors and nurses learn from other doctors and nurses, need to be re-shaped. Changing the models is intimately connected to changing our attitudes and beliefs about what is appropriate behaviour. In short, we need to slow down the experts (doctors and nurses) and get them to understand a new learning process, one which is both didactic and experiential.

Palliative care is complex and multidisciplinary. It is not a logical and linear discipline. Hence, conceptualising palliative care is problematic. How can we teach palliative care tutors to teach something which is complex and problematic? A starting point is to reflect on our own beliefs and attitudes to death and dying. Indeed, examining our own spirituality is highly relevant if we are going to teach others to approach palliative care from a holistic perspective. Once we know ourselves what we hold to be central to our belief system, only then can we go on to inspire and effect change in others.

One great barrier to teaching is time. The juxtaposition of patient care on the one hand and teaching (tutors to teach) on the other, is complex. There are also funding implications to what we do and do not do in teaching and learning. Teaching is a time consuming activity. How much time should be devoted to teaching others to teach perhaps is an individual thing, but some core standards need to be set if we are to move beyond informal teaching.

All health care service has educational implications. We must seek out the links between the two. Whenever we do something we should be able to see why we are doing it and what we need to do to make it better. This should apply throughout one's career, probably more so earlier on than later, though the need for continuing professional development applies to even senior staff. In-service education relies on a good relationship between staff, especially seniors and juniors. This relationship needs to be supportive and co-operative not competitive and hierarchic. A unit's culture or climate needs consideration, to become effective in meeting service and educational needs.

Where are we going?

Overcoming barriers

This chapter has discussed where and how palliative care teachers have learned to teach as well as looking at some of the barriers to teaching palliative care tutors to teach. How can these barriers be overcome, to effect change? Palliative care tutors need to be encouraged to share with others the origins of their thought. Health professionals are taught to solve other people's problems. The curative model of medicine teaches something very different to the caring model. The acute model of medicine is not the same thing as chronic palliative care. The caring model is a school of thought which teaches that finding out the physical problems of a patient is secondary to finding out what the patient perceives a their 'actual' problems. Education requires that learners see *why* they need to learn something. Teachers need to develop the skills of:

"recognising that learners quite legitimately have an educational agenda of their own;

"that this agenda might be different from the teacher's agenda;

"that what somebody wants to learn is not necessarily what someone else thinks they need to learn;

"that any difference between a learner's wants and needs must be negotiated and agreed upon;

"that learning is something that can only be accomplished by the learner and not by the teacher;

"that professional learning requires the development of an insight into one's own practice, relating what one does to why one does it (theory-practice), and the ability to evaluate one's own performance.

Another barrier which needs to be overcome is getting health professionals to admit in the first instance, that barriers exist. Tutors need to be encouraged to see problems and move towards solving them. When one is enthusiastic about a subject, barriers such as anxiety and fear can be overcome. Teachers need to be seen as positive role models if they are effectively to train tutors. Coupled with this, is an understanding that teaching and training are ongoing processes. As James Calderhead discussed in his keynote address on Professional Learning, teachers learn in developmental stages. The professional learner will re-visit many times where he has come from and where he is going By keeping up with the subject matter being taught barriers to learning and training others can be overcome.

Principles for teaching palliative care tutors to teach

Training tutors to teach requires an understanding that learning is about both facts and application. One is not exclusive of the other. Indeed, if the one teaching the tutor to teach does not actively practice what he is teaching, he cannot expect to be a good example to tutors. It is finding the appropriate balance between theory and practice discussed earlier, which includes the learner's desired outcomes in the goals of the programme.

Ongoing evaluation is an essential principle to teaching palliative care tutors to teach. The instructor himself must be prepared to be unprepared, which relates to the earlier point that not knowing something does not necessarily mean loss of control. What is being taught must be relevant. This may seem a simplistic statement, but the original thoughts of the tutor are highly relevant. Allowing tutors to see what they already know will give them confidence and allow them to express their own fears and doubts about teaching. Multiple methodologies, such as role playing, workshops, didactic teaching, and so on need to be encouraged. As palliative care is multidisciplinary so too must the teaching of it be varied. As was stated earlier, few have any formal teaching, hence, teaching tutors to properly prepare themselves both in terms of their subject matter and in the use of equipment such as overhead and slide projectors, is necessary

5.

PROBLEMS IN CONCEPTUALISING PALLIATIVE CARE

Mary Pennell and Suzanne Skevington

The focus of the Conference is on the teaching of palliative care but it is recognised that in order to teach anything, the teaching may be more effective if the concepts underlying the topic are clear. This chapter will examine possible problems with the conceptualisation of palliative care and the way forward in response to the concerns expressed.

It appears axiomatic that those people involved in the medical care of others will be seeking their relief from disease and their cure from illness. Medical school training may build on this philosophy in order to give their students the confidence and courage to go onto the wards and into the community and practice curative medicine. When doctors work with patients in a palliative phase of care, there may be real problems about letting go of the curative ethos, and accepting that care, with death as the appropriate end of the care episode, will be quite acceptable. Closely allied to this is the notion that all of us will die and that death is normal. It should be said, perhaps, that while the act of death is normal, the time of dying will be unique to each patient and this may be the first concept of palliative care that causes unease.

Palliative care has several images attached to it. The connotations of caring for the dying may have imbued it with a certain 'golden glow', because of the frequently heard remark that those doing such work must be exceptional people. As a result, criticising those involved in palliative care may be seen as inappropriate. This can result in difficulties with communication between those who have concerns or little knowledge about palliative care and those who could help them resolve their concerns about the concepts involved. Furthermore, there can be a pride amongst those offering palliative care that suggests that if this model of care is so good, why is it not standard medical practice? The reasoning behind such a bold and logistically impossible step is that palliative care encourages the view of the person as a whole. It attempts to balance the concern for the physical being with care for the social, spiritual and emotional facets of the person as well.

When any group attempts to defend its practice, there is a tendency to stake out the moral high ground. In practice, most practitioners in the health professions would assert they attend to the whole person. By too vigorous an assertion of this point, palliative care workers might alienate those whom they were trying to educate. Where palliative care may differ is that if the physical body seems to be resisting attempts at cure, the concept of palliative care may give the professional carer more overt permission to readily address other issues in ways that might not be considered while curative treatment is still being attempted.

What follows from this is a consideration of the difference between palliative care and the palliative approach to care. It may be that palliative care is that care offered by palliative care specialists, whilst the approach to care using palliative care as the underlying philosophy is the approach that most health care professionals would claim to offer. It is not mere semantics to discuss the difference between these terms or the difference between palliative medicine and palliative care, terms which often appear interchangeable but which may have different emphasis. Medicine has been defined as the art or science of prevention or cure of disease, where care suggests someone offering professional solicitude for another person. The definition of medicine suggests activity and a real sense of 'doing', based on scientific knowledge. The idea of being concerned or solicitous on another's behalf may not appear so satisfying or useful. It may be anathema to people trained for the doing of cure, rather than the giving of care. The fact that these terms have both gained credence in palliative care suggests a possible dichotomy of thought about the basic concept of palliative care within palliative care itself. If those who work within the specialty have difficulty in identifying the underpinning philosophy, how much harder must it be for those outside it.

While it may be accepted that palliative care has much to offer as a philosophy of care, there are some implications that continue to militate against its acceptance in practice. The ethos of winning, as experienced at medical schools, has been referred to earlier. It is worth adding that, by and large, it is the successful student who gains entry to medicine. For some of these doctors, the pain of failure, that is a patient's death, may lead them to protect themselves from such pain by seeing the patient as a collection of symptoms that require attention. By contrast, in attempting to acknowledge the patient as a person first, the palliative care workers leave themselves open to loss, pain and ethical quandaries that do not make for easy practice.

A further concern may be the utilisation of other people's knowledge. Whether it is openly acknowledged or not, most professions have members who find the involvement of other workers in their patients' care difficult, if not impossible. To hand over that care or to ask for the help of a perceived 'expert' at such a vulnerable time for doctor, patient and family may not be possible. When not actively involved with terminal care, it may be easier to discuss the belief that palliative care is about concepts, not practice as in the often quoted remark 'hospice is a philosophy, not a building'. When faced with decisions about seeking help from palliative care consultants or clinical nurse specialists, the specific practices in palliative care may prove to be real stumbling blocks.

A final point to consider with which to conclude this part of the chapter is that for many people, palliation is inextricably linked with quality of life; it might even be said that attention to quality of life gives palliative care its main *raison d'etre*. Such a close alliance is highlighted by the World Health Organisation definition:

"the active total care of patients whose disease is not responsive to curative treatment. Control of pain, of other symptoms and of psychological, social and spiritual problems is paramount. The goal of palliative care is achievement of the best quality of life for patients and their families. Many aspects of palliative care are also applicable in the course of illness in conjunction with anti-cancer treatment."
(WHO, 1990)

In order to offer quality of life, it is imperative that the achievements making up that quality are those chosen by the patient, with the family and professional carers only acting as sounding boards and facilitators, rather than instigators. The concept of total patient care certainly lends itself to such attention to quality of life, but may seem a counsel of perfection that is daunting in its implications for those considering the adoption of a palliative care approach. It is perhaps the breadth of palliative care that is called into question here. If each person receiving palliative care is seen as a whole person and his goals for living underpin his treatment, is such an approach possible for every person in the terminal phase of their illness.

This begs the question of what a terminal illness is, an issue too big to be discussed here. In addition, at what point on the illness continuum can and should such care be offered. It may be that the scale of such care, which can be extremely costly, particularly in terms of time and manpower, means that uncomfortable decisions may have to be made about the numbers and types of patients entering a palliative care programme. There is evidence that in the USA, such questions are being attempted to be answered by legislation with resulting confusion and pain, both within the speciality and without.

Thus far, there has been a concentration on palliative care as an idea and an outline of some noted difficulties about clarifying the concept. The remainder of this chapter will consider possible ways forward for easing the acceptance of palliative care, working on the assumption that palliative care as a concept has much to offer health workers and those for whom they care.

Several earlier references have been made to palliative care and its emphasis on terminal illness, dying and death. It seems clear that an important step forward may be a comfortable acceptance of the idea that we are all going to die. While there may be some concern that the hospice movement causes perhaps an unnecessary medicalisation of a normal process, it has certainly allowed death and dying to be discussed and considered in a way not thought possible in very recent memory.

There is still a way to go, however. If palliative care is limited to patients with a life-threatening disease that fits into some arbitrary category, there will be countless numbers of people who go to their dying without the chance to make sense of their situation and to have attention paid to their whole needs. As a result, the first consideration may be to let death fall back into some more appropriate place in the balance between living and dying. This is not to dismiss the very human fears we have of the unknown nature of death and its aftermath; it is to allow health professionals to work towards the dying and death of any patient in a way that recognises the normality of the process. It is also to underline the success of those health workers who achieve the way of dying sought by those in their charge.

A second and undoubtedly problematic area is that of shared working. It cannot be possible for every health care professional to have all knowledge. In palliative care, where the emphasis is on holistic care, the deficits may show up even more. The temptation to hold onto one's specialism may be overwhelming, resulting from fears of being tried and found wanting by fellow professionals or the worry that the omniscient doctor image might be shattered for the patient or carer, if outside help is called in. Furthermore, many professionals would argue that care for the dying is a very special sort of care that includes a unique relationship between patient and professional carer, that may be jealously guarded.

What is interesting about such understandable fears is that they underscore the humanity of the professional. In palliative care, it would appear that in finding the human face of the patient, the same may hold true for the professional carer so that it becomes a little easier to share such personal feelings. Suffice it to say, the concept of shared working may have to be accepted and worked at before it becomes the comfortable norm.

It is in education that the future of palliative care is recognised as lying. There is a clear understanding that palliative care needs to be taught at both undergraduate and postgraduate levels, with a belief that the earlier such concepts are introduced, the more chance there is that they may influence practice. However, on a very practical level, it appears that students will focus their revision on what will be likely examination material; palliative care holds a low priority. There is also the caveat that even if professional education included such knowledge, there is no guarantee that the information will be put to practical use. It does appear that only where the practitioner accepts the philosophy underpinning palliative care, will it become a basic tenet of care.

The scope for advancement is less where a specialty is seen as a luxury. In these times of financial constraints, it may be harder to finance palliative care consultant posts. Despite this rather gloomy concern, there is a definite impression that the users of the UK National Health Service, for example, are increasingly looking for palliative care and it may be that the demand will be consumer led and therefore powerful - time will tell.

Finally, those involved in palliative care may have to be ready to be flexible in their approach. Any new idea or change of emphasis may cause worry on the part of those who must change. It is a truism to say that change is painful but if the palliative care is in some measure about pain control, then easing the pain of other health care workers may need to be part of the brief. They may also need to be more knowledgeable and more enthusiastic about the whole concept than perhaps is always realised. Such expectations put an extra burden on those working in the field of palliative care, but if the belief about its worth is sincere, the energy to accept the task of clarifying and educating others will be found.

6.

MULTIPROFESSIONAL LEARNING

Mary Thomas and Penny Mimmack

Introduction

Palliative care is a relatively new specialty that has developed over a fairly short period of time, necessitating the laying down of a sound educational foundation. Saunders (1992) maintains that effective education is essential to support the development of effective palliative care. This new specialty needs confident professionally credible and reflective practitioners. It also needs individuals whose broader vision of palliative care is achieved in part through a greater understanding and experience of multiprofessional collaboration.

Professionals who have had an opportunity to work in multiprofessional teams may develop different working practices from those who work more in isolation. The teamworking climate encourages more confidence and perhaps a greater insight into the special skills of other practitioners. This may lead to more effective practice as professionals collaborate with the patient and carers in order to provide quality care. Associated with multiprofessional working may be the concept of the key worker rather than an automatic team leader.

Does personality play a part in creating teams? Perhaps individuals who enjoy working collaboratively self-select whereas for some this type of collaboration feels very threatening.

If we accept that multiprofessional working in palliative care is one of the important educational issues then we need to address the effectiveness of multiprofessional learning as a strategy to promote multiprofessional collaboration. This paper reflects some of these issues and explores some of the challenges of multiprofessional learning in palliative care. The challenges include the following.

"When should multiprofessional learning take place, for example, undergraduate, vocational, postgraduate?

"What strategies should be used to facilitate multiprofessional learning, for example, workshops, study days, problem-based learning, team learning in clinical groups?

41

Challenges in multiprofessional learning and how to begin to meet them

If multiprofessional learning begins when professionals are already qualified, we may need to consider the educational climate in which these different professionals were originally trained. The educational philosophy that underpins the training of doctors and social workers can be quite different and needs to be considered when designing learning opportunities. For some professionals open negotiated learning strategies may be inappropriate or threatening if previous learning has been associated with a more didactic and teacher centred approach.

Each professional discipline develops its own individual vision of the world and this is often associated with different perceptions of patient or client problems. It is often these differences that enrich the team perceptions and enhance quality care. However, they can also be associated with mis-communication and the undervaluing of another professionals' contributions. The challenge is when do we address these issues and in what way? Do we need more innovative approaches to facilitating team learning?

With limited resources multiprofessional learning may not be seen as a priority by many managers. There is no direct evidence to prove that team working is the answer to providing quality care. We assume it to be so. There is not always great motivation to attend multiprofessional courses or design undergraduate curricula which include shared learning with other disciplines. If assessment is 'the tail that wags the dog' then we may need to look at influencing curricula and building strategies that will assess team working skills. Competence in the area of teamworking may need to be achieved in order to become a qualified practitioner or to work in particular types of practice.

Is multiprofessional learning just about bringing different professionals together to learn and expecting that better team working can result? Is it effective to bring different professionals from different teams to a workshop and expect them to return to act as change agents in their own team without support? We really need to define the nature of multiprofessional learning and look at how we can measure outcomes in terms of team practice.

Can the need to gain qualifications, especially in a shrinking job market, be used to promote the development of a new series of multiprofessional qualifications? Is this an area where palliative care educationalists may have special skills?

Can palliative care practitioners jointly learn with professionals working in other contexts and use this experience to build better

42

working practices? Palliative care practitioners need to become aware of how other professionals perceive them and why this may influence collaboration between practitioners working in different settings than palliative care.

Does it make a difference to multiprofessional learning towards team working if the team into which the professional ultimately works is not egalitarian? Recent political changes in primary health care have meant that certain professional groups have lost their discipline specific management structure and are now directly employed by general practitioners? What impact does this have on the educational strategies that will encourage collaboration?

How can we promote continued team development as part of a learning based strategy? If we are encouraging teams to reflect more closely on their collaborative working we may need to be encouraging the development of facilitators working as part of clinical teams. These facilitators will support the continued development of the team both in terms of knowledge of roles as well as developing awareness of individuals within teams.

How can the specialist units in palliative care validate and market their multiprofessional courses in a climate of financial constraints? Networking as well as pooling of resources between these specialist units may well enhance the quality and creativity of the multiprofessional learning opportunities in palliative care. Ensuring that courses are evaluated appropriately and are designed to meet the individual learning needs of professionals will ensure that courses are credible. The linking of hospice education departments with colleges of nursing or higher education institutions, using these bodies to validate courses or collaborate in their production may enhance the effectiveness of courses based in specialist centres.

Will the joint training of teachers of different disciplines or the training of single discipline teachers in multiprofessional learning strategies promote curriculum change for undergraduate or basic training programmes?

Can we encourage the gap between theory and practice to be bridged by developing educational strategies that support reflection on practice? Will we need to encourage the development of good facilitation skills in educationalists and practitioners involved in training in order to promote this strategy?

References

Saunders, C (1992) Voluntary euthanasia, *Palliative Medicine*, 6 (1), 1-5.

7.

RESPONSES TO THE KEYNOTE SPEAKERS

Summarised by Roderick MacLeod

The conclusion of the seminar was provided by the immediate reflections of the two keynote speakers. Neil MacDonald emphasised the importance of identifying appropriate role models in both learning and teaching; as he put it 'specific individuals who did it right'. He reinforced the feeling of the day that palliative care has to move outside the 'end of life' concept and should begin to influence the whole trajectory of illness in medical and nursing care. The need to encourage and foster the development of palliative care in university courses at undergraduate and postgraduate levels was apparent. One effective way of doing this is by close collaboration with the growing field of medical and nursing bioethics. The necessity of collaborative teaching in this and other areas was pointed out.

He identified some of the areas that were not discussed that he felt were of importance. The need for educational research not only to help in our development of teaching but also by reflection to influence the provision of 'good doctors and nurses'. He talked of the need to improve and advance our use of information technology and informatics and linked this with the process of continuing education and re-accreditation. He reminded us of the importance of independent and self-motivated learning.

James Calderhead spoke of the striking number of parallels between his experiences in education and the issues raised during the day. From those experiences he gave examples of the difficult job of helping students to understand some apparently simply concepts of teaching and learning that perhaps had not been apparent because of the difference between their own learning styles and strategies that were very different to those that they were teaching. Another parallel he identified was between teaching teacher training in schools and in palliative care practice. Schools of Education in universities have had to develop intensive programmes to train mentors for training teachers in schools. One of the difficulties in most programmes is to help the mentor recognise the basis of their expertise. He reminded us that one of the difficulties in the mentor/student relationship is that the mentor is not, at times, aware of the enormous amount they know and the student teacher is not aware of what they do not know and are unable to ask. He then addressed the difficult issue of tackling the nature of what expertise is and underlined the complexity of the whole issue. He acknowledged the feeling of the seminar of the complexity of this subject.

Finally he outlined tensions that were apparent from the day that were familiar to him as an educationalist. The tension between assessment and facilitation and the negotiation of a relationship that will foster a worthwhile professional development experience within that tension. He referred to the tension between the need to be reflective practitioners and active practitioners. He underlined the tension between having a prescribed curriculum and a negotiated curriculum pointing out that we will all come to this area from different directions and will bring different skills and attitudes with us. He reminded us finally that long term practices that are brought by the learners to palliative care are valuable to all of us working in this field both as clinicians and as educators. They help us to address the complex challenges to pushing forward education of palliative care in a systematic and gradual way.

8.

TEACHING AND LEARNING IN PALLIATIVE CARE:

FUTURE CONSIDERATIONS

Chris James and Roderick MacLeod

Many issues were raised during the seminar, almost all of which have significant implications for palliative care education. Not surprisingly these, in turn, raise further questions which, in time, need to be addressed. In many ways of course this reflects the rationale for the conference. There are many educational issues in and around palliative care which remain problematic and while this is the case, there will be many unanswered - and perhaps unanswerable - questions.

The purpose of this section is to revisit some of the issues raised in the discussion groups and by the keynote speakers during the day and reported here, to explore those issues further and to raise any other relevant questions for future consideration. There are three key areas which understandably reflect the focuses of the three discussion groups: teaching and learning in palliative care; conceptualising palliative care; and multidisciplinary practice in palliative care.

Teaching and learning in palliative care

A crucial question which comes under the heading 'teaching and learning in palliative care' is: 'What exactly is the nature of learning in palliative care?'. Asking this apparently facile question of palliative care does not mark it out as unique as a domain of professional practice or even professional medical care practice. It can be asked of almost any area of professional knowledge. However, it can be argued that the nature of palliative care makes it a particularly difficult question to answer. However, leaving that question unanswered creates many difficulties for those concerned with education in palliative care.

An exploration of the nature of teaching and learning in palliative care raises a number of important questions.

There are those questions which are relevant to the content of palliative care. Here are some examples.

What is the balance between content and process of palliative care - the knowing that and the knowing how?

--How is education in palliative care best organised?

--Is it adequate to assert that learning about palliative care is so complex, interconnected, personal, idiosyncratic, unpredictable and multidimensional that we must attack it on all fronts using all the methods available?

--Which domains of professional knowledge are most important - the technical? the practical? the moral/ethical? the social, political and economic? the personal?

--Palliative care cannot be seen simply in terms of skills and knowledge that we would associate with cognition; metacognitive, reflective processes must also play a part.

--What is the content of palliative care education and what are the content priorities?

--How can we easily communicate the life-world and culture of palliative care to those wishing to learn, when the settings of palliative care are so diverse?

--Is there an accepted view of the social, political and economic aspects of palliative care that should be taught?

There are other questions which are germane to a consideration of the assessment and evaluation of palliative care education. Examples of these include the following.

How do we measure quality in palliative care education if we are uncertain about the nature of palliative care?

--What criteria might we use when judging the quality of palliative care education?

--Which forms of evaluation are most appropriate?

--How can effectiveness - let alone efficiency - be established when notions of appropriateness remain contested in palliative care education?

--How do we assess learning outcomes in palliative care?

--How do we assess metacognition and reflection in palliative care?

There are also important questions which are concerned with individual learning needs in palliative care. These include the following.

What are the learner's individual needs and how best are they to be identified?

--What personal knowledge does the learner bring to the task of learning about palliative care and how does it influence her/his learning?

--How do palliative care educators recognise and acknowledge the learner's natural orientation to learning?

--What are an individual's barriers to learning and how might they be overcome?

--What are the different learning needs of those from the diverse groups that participate in palliative care?

--What limits should be put on a requirement to confront personal issues in an individual's education in palliative care?

How do palliative care educators reach a balance between individual need and 'course' requirements?

The conceptualisation of palliative care

The fact that palliative care is inadequately conceptualised is a significant challenge for educators because it is not clear which view of palliative care is most appropriate in palliative care education. For example, one view of palliative care - an analytical conception sees it as susceptible to being separated out into the different component parts. Another, contrasting view, sees it as a holistic activity where palliative care is viewed as a complete entity, the value of which will be destroyed by any attempt to disentangle the constituent elements. If the former view is taken a number of questions are raised.

How might palliative care be appropriately disaggregated for educational purposes?

--What are the constituent parts of palliative care?

--How discrete are the different elements of palliative care?

--What is lost of the essential nature of palliative care by the process of disaggregation?

If the latter view is taken and palliative care is viewed as - and only as -a whole a different but equally difficult set of questions emerge.

Where is the most appropriate educational starting point?

--What is the best way of starting the educational task?

--How is the task of learning holistic palliative care to be structured? What is the best route?

--How can a worthwhile curriculum be created?

--How can formative assessment be focused so as to help the learner?

An important tension in the conceptualisation of palliative care is that - put simply - between 'care' and 'cure'. Fundamentally - and again simply - this is a consequence of the relationship between palliative care and palliative medicine. Typical conceptions of 'medicine' with connotations of intervening, controlling and curing may not be as appropriate in palliation as in other kinds of medicine. On the other hand conceptions of care as used in other settings such as general nursing may also be inappropriate.

One of the consequences of the relative 'newness' of palliative care and the diverse settings in which it takes place is that it is difficult to identify a body of knowledge which represents that shared by the profession. Without this accepted body of knowledge, the task of the educator becomes much more difficult.

Another barrier to conceptualising palliative care is that it is about things that we may not naturally consider or link. These include for example, our own death, how we view happiness, wellness and well-being, our view of loss of dignity and being dependent, our individual view of the meaning of life, of sexuality and spirituality. For the carer these disparate concepts will be entangled with the pain and inevitability of failure, the inability to cure and the constant sense of loss.

From our understanding of other forms of knowledge, we know that the form in which any domain of knowledge is communicated shapes our view of it. For example, one problem that novice teachers face is that they may have experienced the subject matter they are required to teach for example geography, history or science, in a very different form. One danger of our enthusiasm and desire to improve teaching and learning in palliative care is that our approach to teaching will unduly shape the conceptualisation of palliative care before it has been adequately formed from the shared experience of practitioners.

Multidisciplinary practice in palliative care

The multidisciplinary nature of palliative care has important educational implications.

Although it must be recognised that palliative care draws on the expertise of the disciplines which typically contribute to palliative care in practice, there is a danger that it will be viewed as being made up solely from the contributions of the different disciplines. There is a tension for the palliative care educator of educating about a body of professional knowledge - palliative care, which is in essence unidisciplinary, and educating about the multidiscplinary nature of palliative care. The tension between these two raises some important questions.

What exactly is multidisciplinary palliative care?

--Which elements should be unidisciplinary and which should be multidisciplinary?

--Who teaches what? Should teaching be multidisciplinary too?

--Should we distinguish between multidisciplinary and interdisciplinary practice?

--Should multidisciplinary palliative care education accept or challenge established relationships between the disciplines?

--Which qualities in individuals facilitate multidisciplinary practice? How are these best acquired?

One final point that should be made is that for all palliative carers, part of the educational process for them is a formulation of their own personal practical knowledge of palliative care on which their practice as educators is founded. For all those learning palliative care and indeed all those teaching palliative care, this involves a fundamental review and appraisal of their own thoughts, feelings, beliefs and actions, some of which are deeply personal. Given the personal nature of the knowledge on which practice is based, there is a case for arguing that *the* issue in palliative care education is not one of learning about palliative care nor indeed one of learning in palliative care but is one of learning through palliative care.

1. *Notes on Contributors*

Speakers

Editors

Interest Group Facilitators & Reporters

2. *Participants*

3. *Blank pages for your own notes.*

CONTRIBUTORS

Keynote speakers

Neil MacDonald is the Alberta Cancer Foundation Professor of Palliative Medicine in the Department of Medicine in Alberta, Canada. He is a leading figure in palliative care research and education both in Canada and throughout the world, and is one of the editors of the *Oxford Textbook of Palliative Medicine.*

James Calderhead is Professor of Education at the University of Bath, UK. Throughout the 1980s his research interests included an investigation of teachers' thinking and he has contributed much to the literature on the decision making of teachers in classroom situations. He is an acknowledged expert in the fields of professional knowledge and the nature of professional learning and has published widely in these areas.

Organisers and editors of this text

Roderick MacLeod is currently Medical Director of the Mary Potter Hospice Foundation in Wellington, New Zealand, having previously been Medical Director at Dorothy House Foundation in Bath. Whilst in Bath he developed his interest in teaching and learning in palliative care and is now researching how doctors learn to care for the dying.

Chris James is Lecturer in the School of Education at the University of Bath. There he teaches in education management and teacher education. His research interests include educational management, teachers' professional learning, nurse education and education in palliative care.

INTEREST GROUP FACILITATORS AND REPORTERS

TEACHING PALLIATIVE CARE TUTORS TO TEACH

Facilitator: **Colin Coles** is Director of Medical Education at the University of Southampton. He has instigated considerable change in the teaching in many hospitals in the Wessex Region with an innovative programme to help medical teachers develop learner-centred educational methods. His research interests have included the relationships between curriculum and learning in undergraduate medical education, curriculum evaluation and elaborated learning in undergraduate medical education.

Reporter: **Kim Rogers** is the Education Manager of the Macmillan Education Centre of the Dorothy House Foundation in Bath. She is interested in the global development of palliative care.

PROBLEMS IN CONCEPTUALISING PALLIATIVE CARE

Facilitator: **Suzanne Skevington** is a health psychologist and Senior Lecturer in the School of Social Sciences in the University of Bath. She has recently completed a book on pain that will provide an additional dimension to our understanding of a symptom that occupies much thought and investigation in palliative care. She has also undertaken research into the understanding of breathlessness and is one of the principal investigators in the development of the WHO Quality of Life Instrument.

Reporter: **Mary Pennell** is a Macmillan Nurse at the Dorothy House Foundation in Bath. She is currently studying the chronically ill patient's experience of trust within the nurse/patient relationship.

MULTIPROFESSIONAL LEARNING

Facilitator: **Mary Thomas** is Lecturer in Medical Education at the Centre for Medical Education, University of Dundee. One of Mary's main research interests is multiprofessional learning. She is the author of a book on the development and improvement of the primary health care team (a project funded by the Scottish Home and Health Department). She was a key member of the team that put together 'Unite the Team', a computer package to assist multiprofessional learning in palliative care. Her thesis for the degree of Master of Medical Education was also in this area.

Reporter: **Penny Mimmack** is a Macmillan Nurse at the Dorothy House Foundation in Bath. She is currently studying the role of the Macmillan nurse as educator.

PARTICIPANTS:

Anne BROWN, Macmillan Nurse Consultant
Education Centre, "D" Floor
Basingstoke District Hospital
Aldermaston Road
Basingstoke, Hants RG24 9NA

James CALDERHEAD Professor of Education
University of Bath
Claverton Down
Bath BA2 7AY

Ian CAPSTICK Consultant Medical Director
St Peter's Hospice
St Agnes Avenue
Knowle, Bristol BS4 2DU

Prue CLENCH Director
Thames Valley Hospice
Pine Lodge, Hatch Lane
Windsor, Berks SL4 3RW

Colin COLES Senior Lecturer in Medical Education
University of Southampton
Southampton General Hospital
Tremona Road
Southampton SO9 4XY

Judy DALE Medical Advisor
St.Richard's Hospice Foundation
Rose Hill House
Rose Hill, London Road
Worcester WR5 1EY

Janet DOYLE Regional Nurse - Continuing Care
East Anglian Regional Health Authority
Union Lane
Cambridge CB4 1RF

Ginny DUNN Macmillan Lecturer in Palliative Nursing
Institute of Nursing
Radcliffe Infirmary
Woodstock Road
Oxford OX2 6HE

Margaret EVANS Macmillan Lecturer in Cancer Nursing
Department of Nursing Studies
University of Southampton
Level C, West Wing
The General Hospital
Southampton SO9 4XY

Hugh FORD Honorary Medical Director
West Norfolk Home Hospice Support
Tapping House
22A Common Road, Snettisham
King's Lynn, Norfolk PE31 7PE

Walter FORMAN   Director, Home Care Services
Veterans Administration Hospital
Albuquerque
New Mexico, USA

Jill GRIFFITHS Education Secretary
Macmillan Education Centre
Dorothy House Foundation
164 Bloomfield Road
Bath BA2 2AT

Laurel HERBST
San Diego Hospice
1117 10th Street
Coronado, Ca 92118, USA

Rachel HERRING Research Officer
Centre for Educational Studies
King's College
Cornwall House Annexe
Waterloo Road, London SE1 8TX

Richard HILLIER Consultant in Palliative Medicine
Countess Mountbatten House
West End
Southampton SO3 3JB

HO SUK MING Nursing Officer
Haven of Hope Hospital
Po Lam Road
Junk Bay, Hong Kong

Hillary HOLMAN Senior Nurse Education
St Peter's Hospice
St Agnes Avenue
Knowle, Bristol BS4 2DU

Georgina HOWES CNS Palliative Care
Palliative Care Team
26 Nassau Street
London W1N 7RF

Val HUNKIN Nurse Consultant
25a Bridge Street
Taunton, Devon TA1 1TQ

Bridget IRVINE Macmillan Tutor
Cambridgeshire College of Health Studies
Education Centre
Hinchingbrooke Hospital
Huntingdon, Cambs PE18 8NT

Cyril IVES Director of Education
Lantern Trust
72 Honey Lane
Waltham Abbey
Essex EU9 3BS

Chris JAMES Lecturer in Education
University of Bath
Claverton Down
Bath BA2 7AY

Peter KAYE Consultant in Palliative Medicine
Cynthia Spencer House
Manfield Hospital
Northampton NN3 1AD

Barry KINZBRUNNER
V itas Healthcare Corporation
100 S. Biscayne Boulevard 1500
Miami, Florida 33131, USA

Mhoira LENG Senior Registrar
Countess Mountbatten House
Moorgreen Hospital
West End, Southampton SO3 3JB

Nikki LE PREVOST Senior Nurse
South Bromley Hospiscare
c/o Orpington Hospital
Orpington, Kent BR6 9JU

Alex LIAMBEY Education Co-Ordinator
St.Margaret's Somerset Hospice
Heron Drive, Bishops Hull
Taunton, Somerset TA1 5HA

Neil MACDONALD Professor of Palliative Medicine
University of Alberta
Edmonton, Alberta
Canada T6G 2J3

Helena MCKINNON Chaplain
Dorothy House Foundation
164 Bloomfield Road
Bath BA2 2AT

Mo MACLELLAN Lecturer in Palliative Care
Princess Alice Hospice
West End Lane
Esher, Surrey KT10 8NA

Rod MACLEOD Medical Director
Dorothy House Foundation
164 Bloomfield Road
Bath BA2 2AT

Dorothy MERRITT
1225 NO Logan (Suite #300)
Texas City
Texas 77590
USA

Penny MIMMACK Macmillan Nurse
Dorothy House Foundation
164 Bloomfield Road
Bath BA2 2AT

Teresa MONTEIRO Macmillan Nurse Consultant
Solihull Healthcare
Berwicks Lane
Marston Green
Birmingham B37 7XR

Ruud ODERKERK Hospice Rozenheuvel
Rosendaalselaan 20
6891 DD Rozendaal
Holland

Karaleela ODERKERK Hospice Rozenheuvel
Rosendaalselaan 20
6891 DD Rozendaal
Holland

Mary PENNELL Macmillan Nurse
Dorothy House Foundation
164 Bloomfield Road
Bath BA2 2AT

Heather PERITON Education Director
Princess Alice Hospice
West End Lane
Esher, Surrey KT10 8NA

Melanie PRATT Vitas Healthcare Corporation
100 S. Biscayne Boulevard 1500
Miami, Florida 33131, USA

Bridget PRESCOTT THOMAS Specialist Nurse Teacher
Flat 3, 5 Ashley Court Road
St.Andrew's, Bristol BS7 9DB

Jennifer RAIMAN Medical Development Advisor
Cancer Relief Macmillan Fund
15-19 Britten Street
London SW3 3TZ

Linda READMAN Macmillan Nurse
Dorothy House Foundation
164 Bloomfield Road
Bath BA2 2AT

Kim ROGERS Education Manager
Macmillan Education Centre
Dorothy House Foundation
164 Bloomfield Road
Bath BA2 2AT

Evelyn SALERNO Vitas Healthcare Corp.,
100 S. Biscayne Boulevard 1500
Miami, Florida 33131, USA

Hilary SALWAY Nursing Director
St Peter's Hospice
St Agnes Avenue
Knowle, Bristol BS4 2AT

John SANDARS RCGP/CRMF Facilitator in Palliative Care
17 Bude Close
Bramhall
Stockport SK7 2QP

Frances SHELDON Macmillan Lecturer in
Psychosocial Palliative Care
The University
Highfield , Southampton SO9 5NH

Suzanne SKEVINGTON Senior Lecturer in Psychology
University of Bath
Claverton Down
Bath BA2 7AY

Debbie SPENCER Macmillan Tutor
St Richard's Hospice Foundation
Rose Hill House
Rose Hill
Worcester WR5 1EY

Mary THOMAS Lecturer in Medical Education
University of Dundee
Ninewells Hospital & Medical School
Dundee DD1 9SY

Loretta TINCKHAM Macmillan Services Development Manager
Cancer Relief Macmillan Fund
15-19 Britten Street
London SW3 3TZ

Richard WALDRON Consultant Physician
"E" Floor
Basingstoke District Hospital
Aldermaston Road
Basingstoke
Hants RG24 9NA

Jeanette WEBBER Chief Nurse Advisor
Cancer Relief Macmillan Fund
15-19 Britten Street
London SW3 3TZ

Terry WILLIAMS Macmillan Nurse
Dorothy House Foundation
164 Bloomfield Road
Bath BA2 2AT

These pages have been added for note-taking purposes.

These pages have been added for note-taking purposes.

These pages have been added for note-taking purposes.

These pages have been added for note-taking purposes.